Just be Nice...
and Other Lost Arts of Etiquette For Management

Just be Nice...
and Other Lost Arts of Etiquette For Management

A Mentor To Those Who Manage People and Expect Productivity and Profitability in Return

Dr. Lawrence G. Knudsen

Writers Club Press
San Jose New York Lincoln Shanghai

Just be Nice…
and Other Lost Arts of Etiquette For Management
A Mentor To Those Who Manage People and Expect
Productivity and Profitability in Return

All Rights Reserved © 2001 by Dr. Lawrence G. Knudsen

No part of this book may be reproduced or transmitted in any form or by any means, graphic, electronic, or mechanical, including photocopying, recording, taping, or by any information storage retrieval system, without the permission in writing from the publisher.

Writers Club Press
an imprint of iUniverse.com, Inc.

For information address:
iUniverse.com, Inc.
5220 S 16th, Ste. 200
Lincoln, NE 68512
www.iuniverse.com

ISBN: 0-595-18233-X

Printed in the United States of America

Contents

List of Illustrations ix
Introduction xi
   Who Should Buy This Book .... *xi*

Part One
Understanding the Basic Principles 1
   CHAPTER ONE
   SHIFTING PARADIGMS 3
      Management Theory *3*
      Business Hierarchy *4*
      Management Etiquette *6*
      Basic Principles of Motivation *7*
      Action Items *9*
   CHAPTER TWO
   THE KEY TO PRODUCTIVITY 13
      A Happy Employee is More Productive *13*
      Management's Role *14*
   CHAPTER THREE
   EMPLOYEE TREATMENT 16
      Treatment of Employees *16*
      Issues and Feelings *18*
   CHAPTER FOUR
   HAPPY EMPLOYEES TAKE CARE OF OUR CUSTOMERS 19
      Poor Service and Lack of Contentment *19*
      Happy Employees Provide Better Service *20*

Chapter Five
Understand Goals of Employment 22
Driving Factors of Employment 23

Chapter Six
Achievement of Employment Goals 25
Helping Employees Achieve Employment Objectives 26
Supporting an Employee's Career Objectives 27
Employees and Mentoring 28

Part Two
Taking Action 29

Chapter Seven
Theory and Reality 31
Theories 31
Reality 32

Chapter Eight
Motivation 34
Motivation Theories 35
Motivation Reality 36
Understand Why People Are Working-Survey 36
Predictive Index 38
Individual Development Plan 39
Discussion with the Employee 41

Chapter Nine
Employee Perceptions and Attitudes 46
Theories on Perceptions and Attitudes 46
Perceptions and Attitudes Reality 47
Keep Employees Informed 49
Listen 50
How Am I Doing Survey 51

Chapter Ten
Management of Group Morale 58
- *Morale and Productivity 59*
- *Morale Theories 59*
- *Morale Reality 60*
- *Equity Among Peers 60*
- *Take Care of Your Employees 62*
- *Become Their Biggest Fan 63*
- *Promote Often 64*
- *Timely Annual Reviews 65*
- *Employee Terminations 66*

Chapter Eleven
Leadership 70
- *Examples of Great Leaders 71*
- *Leaders Without Titles 74*
- *Leadership Theories 75*
- *Bosses and Reality 76*
- *Specific Job Descriptions 77*

Chapter Twelve
Participative Management 84
- *The Office Environment 84*
- *Employees and Production 86*
- *Employee Input 87*
- *Theories of Participative Management 88*
- *Participative Management Reality 88*
- *Participative Management Actions 89*
- *Hire the Best 90*
- *Give Instructions 91*

Provide the Necessary Tools 92
Leave Them Alone 94
Follow-up 95

CHAPTER THIRTEEN

THE MANAGEMENT OF CHANGE 99
Change is Constant 100
Change and Theories 101
Change and Reality 102
The Communication of Change 103
Look Inward Before Counseling Others 106

CHAPTER FOURTEEN

JUST BE NICE 108
Today's Society 108
The Art of Being Nice 110
Employees and Mistakes 112
Other Ways to be Nice 113
Being Nice and Giving Gifts 113
Give It a Shot! 114

CHAPTER FIFTEEN

CONCLUSION 115
Thirty-five Years of Experience 115

Index **121**

List of Illustrations

Ah…hah! 1

Diagram 1 Business Hierarchy-Current Structure 10

Diagram 2 Business Hierarchy-Shifting Paradigms.............11

Diagram 3 Business Hierarchy-Knudsen's Paradigm 12

Action 29

Sample Exhibit I-Personal Attributes Survey.......................42

Sample Exhibit II-Individual Development Plan 44

Why You Need to Understand
    Why Your Employees Are Working! 45

Sample Exhibit III How Am I Doing Survey 54

Why You Need to Listen While Your Employees Are Speaking! 56

Why A "How Am I Doing Survey" Must Be Done Anonymously
    and Without Recrimination! 57

Bob Being Acknowledged by His Boss! 69

Sample Exhibit IV Job Description 79

Sample Exhibit V Performance Review 81

Why You Need Very Specific Job Descriptions
    and Performance Reviews! 83

Sample Exhibit VI Job Description-Required Equipment 96

Why You Need to Follow Up After Delegating! 98

A ONE MINUTE ANALYSIS OF MANAGEMENT ETIQUETTE...117

Introduction

Who Should Buy This Book

Just be Nice…and other forms of etiquette for management is a "*How-To*" book that mentors those who manage people and expect productivity and profitability in return. In so doing:

- It provokes thoughtful consideration about employment treatment.
- It motivates readers to think before acting towards their employees.
- It teaches that if your employees are not happy then your customers are not receiving the proper care that they deserve; that you cannot properly take care of your customers with an unhappy workforce.

With over thirty-five years of experience in various management positions including that of a consultant, educator, and public speaker, I have successfully managed personnel in general management, operations, accounting, personnel, information technology, marketing, sales and lending. It is this experience that I draw upon to compare the theories of management taught in the Business Schools to what actually works in the workplace.

This book addresses a serious subject with subtle and sometimes not so subtle humor and helps address the following questions:

- What are the motivating factors that when satisfied will create happy employees at no expense to the company?
- What are the steps that need to be taken to create a happy and productive workforce?
- Why do these steps work?

My experience has shown that management understands the importance of happy employees and what they can do for the company but is so busy doing *business things* that a contented workforce is left to chance.

This book is intended to be used as a supplement to formal and informal on the job training of management personnel. Over twelve million large and small companies do business in the United States alone. All of these businesses have several layers of management and those who aspire to be managers who are struggling to get the most productivity out of the workforce that they manage or hope to manage in the future.

Several books on business etiquette can be found; however, most of these deal with the subject of how to do business in other countries and how to conduct yourself with other business associates. There is no other resource that deals with the etiquette involved in the management of personnel. This book fills this void!

Part One
Understanding the Basic Principles

CHAPTER ONE

Shifting Paradigms

"The problem, when solved, will be simple."
Anonymous

As I was growing up, I was taught to say thanks, please, to eat with the proper fork, to treat elders with respect and other forms of etiquette that would help me succeed in society. Then as I matured, I always referred to these teachings because they had been passed down from generation to generation and had actually worked quite well.

Management Theory

In my professional life, as I moved into management, I was taught management theory: not etiquette, but teachings that sounded good and would make you feel good about yourself, but failed to achieve any change in the personnel that I managed. So armed with this limited knowledge, I resolutely went forward to manage personnel and try to receive some measure of productivity and profitability. I practiced these theories but got discouraged because I saw no measurable results. It was then I figured that, *as with life, there **must** be certain practices or etiquette that when followed will lead to behavioral changes in personnel that will benefit both them and the organization for which they work.*

Business Hierarchy

During my formative years in business, I was also led to believe that the Hierarchy of Business, or pecking order, consists of five basic *groups* that share in the success of the company. (See diagram 1.)

At the top of this pyramid you will find the *shareholders*. The group of shareholders holds the most important position because they have placed their capital at risk so that the other four groups can share in the company's success. Without them there would be no business hierarchy, no customers, no employees, no taxes paid to the communities, no business relationships with other businesses, and no product. The shareholders must always be held in the highest regard, and all actions taken by personnel should be done with the enhancement of their investment in mind. This is what I was taught and it is also what I believe.

Customers are the second most important group. Obviously, without customers there would also be no business, no return to the shareholders, etc. Customers drive production, staffing needs, expansion, return on investment to the shareholders, product design and marketing. The customer drives all aspect of the business. They can never be taken for granted nor looked upon as a nuisance, just something that needs attention. How a business takes care of its customers is synonymous with profitability: the creation of enthusiastic and contented shareholders.

Number three on the Business Hierarchy chart is the *employee,* the resource of the company that gets things done, that satisfies the shareholders. This group is also at the forefront of product design, marketing, accounting, planning, working with regulators, budgeting and production; and foremost, they are the group that works with the customer on a continuous basis through sales, training, support, conflict resolution and production. This is the group, via their actions, that can create satisfied customers or send them to the competition. While they are an expense, they are also the most important resource the company has.

The fourth group-the *communities*—produce the labor force and share in the success of the company by receiving taxes and benefits from events surrounding the employees of the business such as home construction, consumer spending, education and recreation.

The fifth and final group is what I call the *"stakeholders".* This group comprises the businesses and individuals that do business with the company. This might include insurance and advertising agencies, accounting firms, form suppliers, transportation and technology companies, etc. An analysis of the accounts payable system will demonstrate the very numerous companies that are paid significant sums every year from the business for services rendered. They also have a notable interest in the success of the company.

After working within the aforementioned business hierarchy for several years, I began to note a definite shift within this paradigm. (See diagram 2.) *The role of the employees in an organization replaced the customers as the second most important group* (See diagram 3.); so now, *the role of management must also shift,* and definite management etiquette for managing employees has to be formed! So, if the employees are not happy and are not receiving the proper attention they deserve, then the customers are not receiving the proper care also. *You cannot properly take care of customers and achieve high levels of productivity with an unhappy work force.*

Management Etiquette

The dictionary[1] defines etiquette "as prescribed forms and practices of correct behavior." This book covers the practices of correct behavior in managing people so that

---

[1] Webster's II New Riverside Dictionary. NY; Berkley Books, 1984

they can respond with maximum effort and productivity. The ideas presented are fundamental, gathered from over thirty-five years of practical experience.

Only a few references will be given to outside sources since the ideas herein are mine and the theories presented are an accumulation and a synopsis from several sources digested throughout my life. This is not to say that others haven't expressed some of the same views on reality, but what I am presenting is an accumulation of my own thoughts and ideas. I believe in them because I have seen them work. I stand by them because they are effective; they have been tested, refined, implemented, and distilled. They come from practical experience, from watching, listening, analyzing, and applying.

They are designed to show that the greatest key to productivity is a happy employee, and show simply how to make employees happy, concluding with the most basic, underlying management concept.

Basic Principles of Motivation

Now, to establish or create an action plan for managing people you must understand the basics of human motivation. Maslow[2], a research psychologist, studied human

---

[2.] Maslow, Abraham. Motivation and Personality. New York, NY: Harper & Row, 1954

motivation and developed what he referred to as the "Hierarchy of Needs". Its basic principle is that the needs of employment are prioritized and that the most basic needs are met first. **He did not, however, show the relationship of productivity with the fulfillment of these needs.** Fulfilling employment needs and employee productivity are not mutually exclusive. Each is intertwined and can permeate the organization if the principles of good management are understood.

When these principles are followed:

- Employees will respond with maximum effort and productivity.
- Customers will be taken care of.
- Satisfied customers will spread word about the company.
- The business will grow.
- Personnel will want to work there.
- Turnover will be low and replacements will be easy to find.
- Training costs will be dramatically reduced.
- Growth of the business will create new jobs.
- The bottom line will improve.

Fulfilling these employment needs then leads us to a discussion of **five basic principles** that should be used in managing human resources. These principles are so basic that they may seem self-evident; however, I believe a review is in order because of the aforementioned shifting paradigm.

Action Items

Also during the following chapters, once the five basic principles are understood and acknowledged, ten action items that are required in recognizing and fulfilling these assumptions will be presented. Current personnel issues that you are now experiencing can and will be solved such as:

- Lack of production.
- Low morale.
- Complacency.
- Inability to get along with others.
- Continual tardiness.
- Constant distraction to others.
- Poor customer service.
- Lack of motivation.
- Continual complaining.
- Poor quality of output.
- Overall poor work habits.

Understanding the principles and following the action items that will be discussed herein will give you the tools to manage people and expect productivity and profitability in return.

10   JUST BE NICE...AND OTHER LOST ARTS OF ETIQUETTE FOR MANAGEMENT

Business Hierarchy

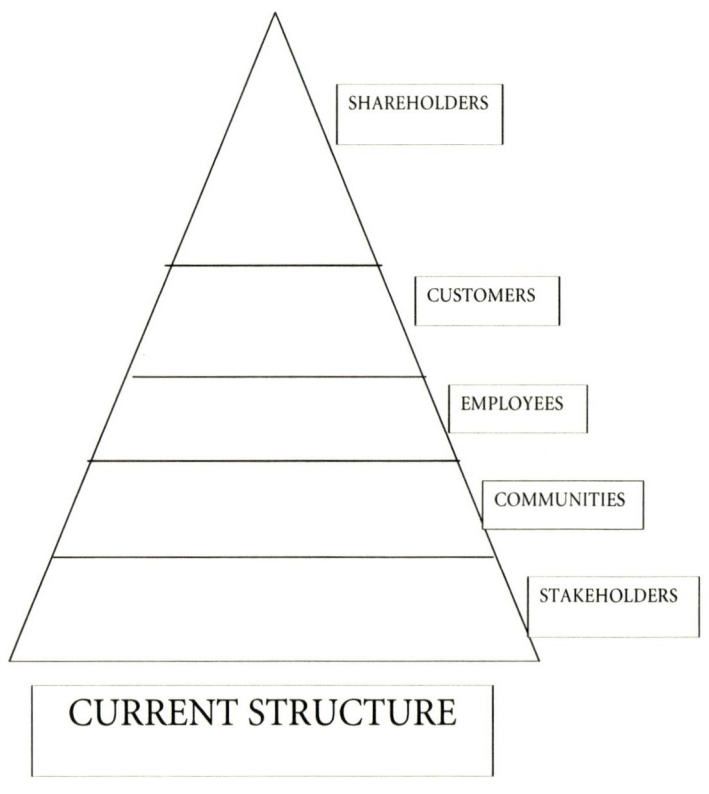

Diagram 1

Business Hierarchy

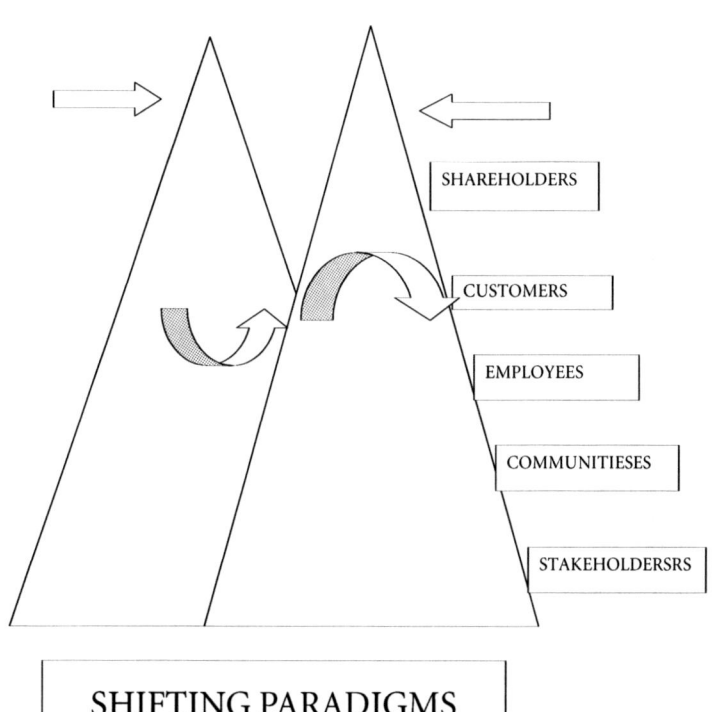

Diagram 2

Business Hierarchy

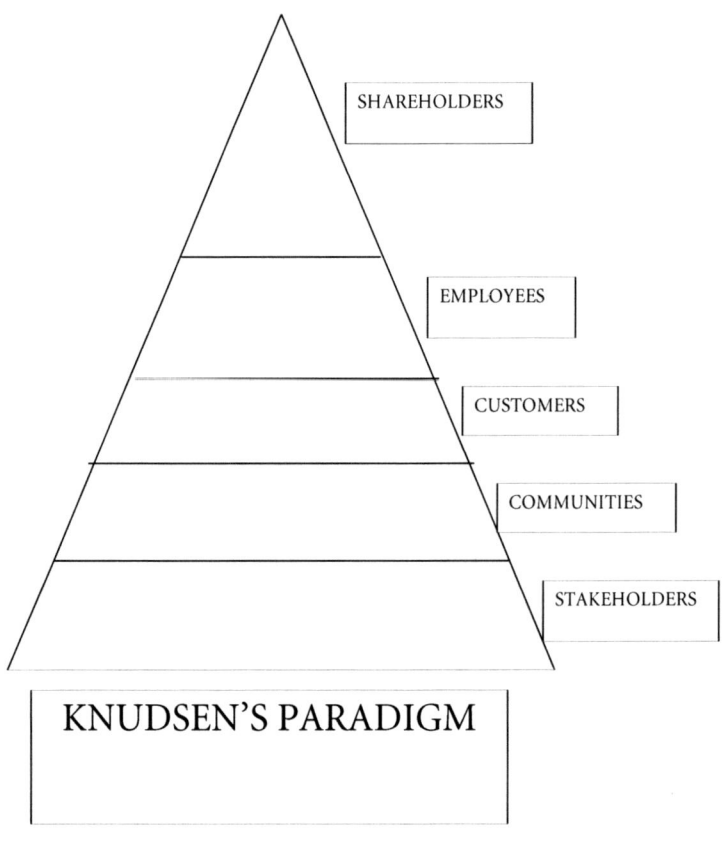

Diagram 3

Chapter Two

The Key to Productivity

"You can't achieve maximum production from an inaccurate understanding of where other people are coming from."

Stephen R. Covey

A Happy Employee is More Productive

PRINCIPLE #1...*The single greatest key to productivity is happy employees!*

This, I'm sure, will cause you some amusement, while at the same time thinking "where is this guy coming from...of course happy employees are more productive. I've known this for years."

I'll be the first to admit that I thought the same way when I first came upon this fact. The problem that I've encountered is that while most people understand this concept, they feel understanding it is sufficient and they take no action to help bring this about. After you hired Bob, for instance, what did you do to insure that he is contented and productive, or did you think that it wasn't your responsibility?

This suggests even more questions that require answers before we can proceed further. If happy employees are more productive, what, if any, is the role of management to bring this about? Shouldn't they make themselves happy? Don't you perform your job better when you are in a good mood? What should management do, if anything, to make them happy?

Management's Role

As to the role of management in the employee's happiness, what happens while at the office is a major factor in persons well being. To many, the job and its attended success is a high priority in their lives. Management can certainly affect the moods of employees in the workplace, and they should. Remember the last time something favorable happened at the office? Ask Bob how he felt when he was given:

- A promotion.
- A good performance review.
- A pat on the back.
- Acknowledgement of a job well done in front of his peers.
- Praise.
- A simple thank you.

Ask yourself as well! Remember how you felt at the time, and how your job performance, productivity, and interaction with other employees, customers and other businesses was affected simply by the euphoria you felt within as a direct result of a positive action taken by management towards you?

Yes, you can influence the happiness of your employees. To understand that happy employees are more productive is important; to take action to bring this about is what proactive management is all about.

Chapter Three

Employee Treatment

> *"The aim of flattery is to soothe and encourage us by assuring us of the truth of an opinion we have already formed about ourselves."*
>
> Edith Sitwell

Up to this point we have learned that the single greatest key to productivity is happy employees. We are now ready to be introduced to the next tenet, i.e....PRINCIPLE #2...*Employee treatment is the key to employee happiness.*

Treatment of Employees

To get a better understanding of this fact, reach back to a time when you were mistreated or felt that you were mistreated while at work. It might have been in the form of criticism, a put down in front of others, a word spoken to you in anger, a feeling of not being appreciated and/or not being considered for a promotion. While any of these events may have been perceived or based upon fact, the truth of the matter is that your productivity during this time and the period of healing afterwards was not at it's highest point. Suffice it to say that you were probably just going through the motions. You were suffering, while at the same time so was the company for which you worked and it's customers.

You probably spent a great deal of time expressing your displeasure with others around you leading to a lack of production on their parts as well. Instead of focusing upon your job, you were probably asking yourself the following questions:

- Why aren't I appreciated?
- Why is my boss such a _____?
- How much longer must I look like I'm working before it's time to go home?
- What do they expect from me around here?
- Why am I always singled out for criticism?

The fact that you are still employed suggests that your overall performance and productivity is satisfactory—while not at that particular time—or that management lacked the skills to address the issue or just refused to do so. Either way, your inner thoughts about the way that you were treated affected your performance for a period of time.

Issues and Feelings

One belief I have experienced over the years is that the way I feel about personal issues is pretty much the same way others feel about the same issues. Believe it or not, but it's true! Now with this understanding, we can be assured that people with whom you work are going to respond to behavior toward them in much the same manner as you would. Hmmm! Think about that for a while as we proceed on to the next chapter and talk about how *good* things happening within the workforce affect customers and productivity in a **positive way.**

CHAPTER FOUR

Happy Employees Take Care of Our Customers

> *"Rather than aiming to dominate or exploit markets, the new mind-set encourages firms to delight customers...just doing the job for customers and satisfying them is no longer enough..."*
>
> The Portable MBA

Poor Service and Lack of Contentment

All of us at one time or another, probably more frequently than we desire, are objects of totally poor, even rude, customer service. Have you ever stood in line at a retail establishment while a sales person talked very loudly to a friend on the phone about events of the previous evening? I expect we all have. What about the attitude of a sales clerk who feels he or she is doing you a favor by helping you? I can tell you've experienced that one too. My overall favorite is that while I'm talking to an employee of a firm about doing business with them, in person, sitting in front of their desk, they will take several telephone calls and treat the caller as more important than I am. My time, in their eyes, is less important than theirs. I'm sure you have had your own experiences with poor customer service, and have a particularly favorite one.

The question that always surfaces in my mind when poor service is encountered is "what is the cause of this poor service?" I'm sure these employees understand and have been taught about the importance of good service, and they feel just like you and I when they receive poor service. Why then do they occasionally provide poor service or productivity? I'm sure they are good, productive and valuable employees and if a complaint is made about them, management would respond by saying, "this doesn't sound like Bob at all".

Happy Employees Provide Better Service

The answer as to why poor service is sometimes given to customers, suppliers, and other employees is found within the next fact…PRINCIPLE #3…*Happy employees take care of our customers and are more productive.*

With this in mind, wouldn't you rather be taken care of by an employee of a company who was just promoted rather than by some one who was just overlooked for the same promotion? How about the choice of being served by someone who just received a good review or a compliment about their work or by someone who's recent review was poor, or whose work was just criticized?

This fact is evident: a happy employee just simply provides better service, and the examples of poor service by a good employee probably happen when an event at work or home created his or her unhappiness.

If you accept the idea that happy employees are more productive and provide exceptional customer service, it then falls to management to do what it can to help the employee achieve happiness at work. How to do this, in very specific terms, will be discussed in future chapters.

Chapter Five

Understand Goals of Employment

"I don't think anybody yet has invented a pastime that's as much fun, or keeps you as young, as a good job."
Frederick Hudson Ecker

I have been in the workforce since I was a young boy. I remember working after school as a paperboy, selling fruit and vegetables door to door, and as I got older working for my father as we installed and finished hardwood floors. It was very simple, if I wanted any spending money I had to work for it. My career objectives were also very simple…if I worked I would get paid. In so doing, I could use my remuneration in exchange for goods and services worldwide. Actually, I spent most of it on candy at the local store when I was younger and on sports equipment and girls as I got older. My entire world at that time was just a few square miles. As long as I was paid I was happy in my work and I would do everything that was expected of me, and do it well. I was happy. Why shouldn't I be? I was achieving everything I set out to accomplish through my employment.

Driving Factors of Employment

Wouldn't it be nice if everyone could share in that same euphoria from employment that I did when I was younger? Actually you can, and so can every employee who works for you. Simply stated, this can be achieved by recognizing the truths of the following axiom in PRINCIPLE #4...*Happiness in employment comes from achieving one's employment goals.*

Now that I am older, the receipt of a salary and benefits is still important to me; however, as my life style changes and certain basic needs are now being met, the driving factors behind my employment needs have changed. I would make Maslow proud. My needs from employment have evolved.

Ask yourself what are the driving factors of your employment? Why do you work? What are the factors in your job that will make you contented? Then just for fun, ask Bob! Are they the same, comparable, or miles apart?

We all have different driving factors concerning employment and they can be contrary to what others might expect. Some of the employment objectives I have encountered in others are:

- Career.
- Second income.
- Break from the house.
- Boredom.
- Prestige.
- Power and influence.
- Money.
- Satisfying others.
- Health insurance.

Understanding why the people who you manage are working, and helping them in the achievement of their employment goals will create this happy employee that will be a better, more productive, employee and will be a great asset to whomever they might touch.

Chapter Six

Achievement of Employment Goals

"Any time you see a turtle atop a fence post, you know it had some help."

Anonymous

As I entered the workforce and worked up the corporate ladder, I always thought it was important that my supervisors understood what my employment goals were. If they didn't ask, I told them. I used the direct approach. Sometimes the results were very interesting, anywhere from a who cares shrug to a surprising "What can I do to help?" response. Naturally, when I received the latter approach, I was elated and responded with a renewed vigor and productivity. Here was a person and an organization that cared about what I wanted, and realized that the achievement of my goals and profitability and productivity for the organization were not at odds with one another, but intertwined.

Helping Employees Achieve Employment Objectives

As I mentioned in the previous chapter, we all have different goals. Treating all employees as though they all have the same objectives is doing a disservice to the work force and the organization. Every employee should be given the opportunity to achieve his or her goals. So, the next and final statement of management doctrine concludes with…PRINCIPLE #5…*Helping people achieve employment objectives creates happy employees; hence, productive employees.*

What if by chance, Bob's goal is to replace you or to achieve a position in the company that is really beyond his reach: Should you still help him? What if his goal is for a position that will require him to move to another company because you don't have positions of that type?

The answer to all of the above questions is a *qualified* yes. It must be understood that while you understand Bob's employment needs and are willing to work with him to help him to achieve these goals, there can be no guarantee that these goals will be met. Circumstances are always changing. You may like your job and don't want to be replaced. Maybe after all of your mentoring, Bob just doesn't have what it takes for his desired goal. However, even with this understanding, your willingness to help will have a positive influence on Bob's work habits.

Supporting an Employee's Career Objectives

As an example, I used to have a graveyard shift computer operator in my employ that was going to school at the time and wanted a career in marketing. He had two years to go to obtain his degree. His work habits were average and his productivity was okay, but not exceptional. Knowing that we would lose his services within two years anyway, I made arrangements with the Director of Marketing to use his talents to supplement her department and fill in when necessary. The computer operator assisted the marketing department on his own time and was not paid any additional salary. This resulted in the following:

- The marketing department's backlog of projects was eliminated, at no additional costs.
- The computer operator gained essential marketing experience that could be applied to his resume.
- The operator became an exceptional employee with high productivity.
- The company saved the cost of adding staff to the marketing department.

Although the company was going to lose this operator in two years, mentoring this employee created a win-win situation for all involved.

Employees and Mentoring

Employees need mentoring. They need to know that someone will help them acquire their employment objectives, if possible. Before we proceed further, let's review…

PRINCIPLE #1…The single greatest key to productivity is happy employees.

PRINCIPLE #2…Employee treatment is the key to employee happiness.

PRINCIPLE #3…Happy employees take care of our customers and are more productive.

PRINCIPLE #4…Happiness in employment comes from achieving one's employment goals.

PRINCIPLE #5…Helping people achieve employment objectives creates happy employees; hence, productive employees.

With an understanding of the basic tenets of managing people, you are ready to proceed to the discussion of how to put these assumptions to work and to achieve this improvement in productivity, profitability and customer service that I have been promising.

Let's go to work!

PART TWO
TAKING ACTION

Chapter Seven

Theory and Reality

"It can be so wonderful, finding out you were wrong…ignorant…know nothing, not squat. You get to start over. It's like snow falling that first time each year."

Rick Bass

Theories

Life teaches a tremendous amount of what I call *stuff*. Good stuff! Bad stuff! In between stuff! Stuff that forms the foundation of great achievements, and stuff which falls apart with the first piece of resistance. Some of the ideas suggest that when certain actions are initiated, responses to those actions are predictable, almost guaranteed.

While attending Business School I was taught theories which differ from guaranteed results because the responses to certain actions were not guaranteed to happen, but it was felt that they would.

When thinking about some of these theories, the theories of X and Y styles of management comes to mind. Paraphrasing them very loosely, one style of management believes that the best way to treat employees is by punishing them when they have performed actions contrary to those of management. The other theory rewards them when they have performed up to or beyond expectations. These theories accomplish the same tasks through very different approaches: *Reward or punishment!*

Theories are only a guide, a source of information to those new in management positions. As experience in managing people and being managed by them grows, these theories are replaced by reality. What *should* work is replaced by what *does* work.

Reality

Have you ever set out to accomplish certain goals where extensive training for a period of time was required beforehand? If you have, when the training had been completed and you were ready to achieve these goals, invariably you will come across someone who has been doing what you are now setting out to do, who will tell you to forget most of the information that you just learned and tell you what you really need to do to be successful.

All of a sudden, theory is being replaced with reality. *What should work is being replaced by what does work:* information that has been given to you by someone who has actually "been there, done that".

In the ensuing chapters, you will be given theories about the following management issues:

- Employee motivation.
- Employee perceptions, attitudes, and communication.
- Group morale.
- Leadership.
- Participative management.
- Management of change.

As I promised, I will also share with you ten reality based action items that really work, replacing these theories with reality by someone who has "been there, done that." That someone would be… ah… me!

These views on reality come from my own experiences and through trial and error. Many thanks go to those who were erred upon and are still speaking to me! These ideas have worked, are now working, and I believe will continue to work in the future!

Chapter Eight

Motivation

> "What's gone wrong? Why do so few companies actually make use of the greatest competitive weapon of all—the powerful resources of motivated, energized, cooperative, trusting people?"
>
> Wickham Skinner

> "If all the air were suddenly sucked out of the room you're in, what would happen to your interest in this book? You wouldn't care about anything except getting air. Survival would be your only motivation. But now that you have air, it doesn't motivate you. This is one of the greatest insights in the field of human motivation: satisfied needs do not motivate. It's only the unsatisfied needs that motivate. Next to physical survival, the greatest need of a human being is psychological survival —to be understood, to be affirmed, to be validated, to be appreciated."
>
> Stephen R. Covey

Numerous theories abound on the subject of motivation. Volumes have been written and grants issued so that this understanding can be acquired. Questions about motivation in employment needing answers are:
- Why do people do what they do?
- How can motivation be exploited?
- Can motivation be turned into profits?
- As a manager, how can it be used?
- What is the single most important action that I, as a manager, can do to motivate my employees?

Motivation Theories

Trying to find answers to the above questions, I culled through several Business School notes and life experiences on the subject and narrowed it down to the following three theories that answer some of the previous questions:

1. The behavior of employees and their productivity depends to a great extent on how well they are satisfying certain needs on the job: physiological, safety, social, esteem, and self-actualization.
2. Motivation is an internal drive that incites the individual to take some kind of action. It is a stimulation to satisfy a need.

3. The supervisor can shape behavior of his or her subordinates by utilizing rewards—the satisfaction of needs—that are at his or her disposal.

Motivation Reality

I really like these theories, probably because they work. But they don't provide specific actions as to what a manager can do to motivate his or her employees. At this point I shall present to you the first of ten action items that turn theory into reality.

ACTION #1—*Understand why people are working and commit to help them achieve these goals.*

Understand Why People Are Working-Survey

This can be a very powerful action on the part of management. You will be overwhelmed with the increase in productivity that will arise from its implementation. There are several ways to accomplish this task. The most common would include a survey (see exhibit I) of each employee in the organization, asking questions such as:

- What are your career aspirations? Immediate, short and long term?
- Do you like to be responsible for the work of others?
- Do you like working with people?
- Do you like to work under pressure?
- Do you like to do several things at once?
- Do you like to sell?
- Are you patient with yourself and others?
- Can you perform tasks according to pre-established guidelines?
- Are you an effective delegater?
- Can you work well with detail?
- Do you like to work on your own without assistance from others?
- Do you like challenges?
- Can you work at a fast pace?
- Are you tolerant of others, and can you accept new ideas?
- Do you like performing repetitive tasks?
- Do you need to work around others?
- Do you like to travel? Can you travel?

The answers to these types of questions help management to ferret out possible conflicts with abilities, strengths and career objectives. You'd be surprised how often career objectives, capabilities and desires of the employee are at odds. After completion of a survey similar to this, a former employee of mine indicated that he wanted a career in management but that he also did not want to be responsible for the work of others. After counseling, he agreed that his desire to move into management was predicated on the fact that he felt that was what all employees should do. He was very happy to learn that you could have a successful career as part of a team, and not necessarily that of a team leader. Helping him see this brought an immediate improvement in morale, contentment, and productivity.

The most important question to be answered, of course, would be—what are your career aspirations? All other questions and answers are used to support the answers to that one question.

Predictive Index

Another tool to be used in assessing the needs of each employee and correlating them with the employee's abilities is a predictive index (PI). Just what is a predictive index anyway? It is a proven system of information gathering which will help assure that you will bring into your organization, promote, and give responsibility to only the most qualified, and to those who *desire* it. (Companies that provide this type of service can readily be found on the Internet by using the search words "predictive index.") These employees will then be developed and managed so as to make them as effective and productive as possible. A predictive index provides managers with specific, relevant knowledge of and insights into the *behavior and potential* of people working under their leadership; ensuring recognition of the importance of people in the development and execution of business plans.

It is done by having the employee complete both sides of a single form asking them to identify characteristics that they associate with themselves and what they perceive other people see as their characteristics as well. It is not a test, and there are no right or wrong answers.

Experience has proven to me that they are very accurate and provide both the employee and the employer with great insights into the driving factors within the employee. Aside from the above, a PI will shed more light and provide more assistance with the process of helping an employee obtain his or her employment objectives than any other tool I have used.

Individual Development Plan

A further method of assistance can be the individual development plan (IDP) (see exhibit II). Once we know where the employee wants to go and that his or her aptitudes are in harmony with that intent, an IDP provides a map of how to get there. It is a *plan of action* for the period covering the employees performance review and is broken down by quarters and updated and reviewed with the employee on an annual basis. It lists the employee's strengths, *with emphasis on the strengths*, along with a few weaknesses that might prevent them from achieving their goals.

I must highlight how important it is to focus on the employee's strengths. It appears to be a normal practice to spend time dwelling on the things that we don't do well, overlooking those areas in which one excels. For instance, I'm reminded of a student who brought home a report card which contained six "A's" and one "C". With no mention of the A's, the student was scolded for not achieving an "A" in a study, like European history, for which the student had no aptitude or interest. His interest was technology, and he excelled in all the subjects that surrounded this topic. This student should have been applauded for acing those areas that are needed for his future.

Discussion of weaknesses in an IDP interview should only dwell on those items that are needed to achieve the employee's goals. If an employee is weak in sales, for instance, but it is not required in their career objective, then it should be discarded. The IDP should *accentuate the positive and minimize the negative.* (This sounds like a good line for a song.) The quarterly action items that both you and the employee are to adopt should be specific, and should include the following:

- Educational opportunities.
- In-house training.

- Product knowledge training.
- Accomplishing specific agreed upon tasks.
- Certain community involvement.
- Habit modification.

Include only the action items that will benefit the employee, and by extension the company, that are very specific and can be measured and quantified. Don't include items such as, "Bob, you need to become a better person". How do you measure something like that? By the number of people he ticked off this week compared to last? Be realistic! The IDP does require work, both on the part of the manager and the employee, but this work is highly leveraged when compared to the results in additional employee performance received.

Discussion with the Employee

One last tool to use in accomplishing ACTION #1, if you don't like any of the above, is a one on one discussion with the employee. Simply ask them what their career objectives are and what can you do to help. You'd be amazed at what a sincere attempt on your part to help the employee will generate in motivation. Try it one day and you will be astonished at the results!

SAMPLE EXHIBIT I
Personal Attributes Survey

January 2000   Employee- Bob

1. What are your career aspirations? Immediate? Short Term? LongTerm?

   Immediate - To make more money.
   Short Term - To make even more money.
   Long Term - To become a Senior Marketing Analyst

		YES	NO
2.	Do you like being responsible for the work of others?		✓
3.	Do you like working with people?	✓	
4.	Do you like to work under pressure?		✓
5.	Do you like to do several things at once?	✓	
6.	Do you like to sell?		✓
7.	Are you patient with yourself and others?	✓	
8.	Can you perform tasks according to pre-established guidelines?	✓	
9.	Are you an effective delegater?		✓
10.	Can you work with detail?	✓	

		Yes	No
11.	Do you like to work with detail?	☑	☐
12.	Do you like to work on your own without assistance from others?	☑	☐
13.	Do you like challenges?	☑	☐
14.	Can you work at a fast pace?	☑	☐
15.	Are you tolerant of others, and can you accept new ideas?	☑	☐
16.	Do you like to perform repetitive tasks?	☐	☑
17.	Do you need to work around others?	☐	☑
18.	Do you like to travel?	☐	☑
19.	Can you travel?	☑	☐
20.	Are you willing to relocate if necessary to obtain your goals?	☑	☐
21.	Do you like to do research?	☑	☐
22.	Do you like to speak in front of others?	☐	☑
23.	Do you like to write?	☑	☐

SAMPLE – EXHIBIT II
INDIVIDUAL DEVELOPMENT PLAN

June 2000-June 2001   Bob
_____   _____
DATE   EMPLOYEE

GOALS

Immediate: _Improve earnings_

Short-term: _Improve earnings_

Long-term: _Senior Marketing Analyst_

_____ACTION ITEMS_____

First quarter: 1. Complete all projects accurately and on time. (as per Job description)
2. Attend enhanced Training on the M.C.I.F.

Second quarter: 1. Tie MCIF with local non-customer data base.
2. Continue to complete all projects on time.

Third Quarter: 1. Add non-core applications to the MCIF.
2. Continue accurate and timely projects.

Fourth Quarter: 1. Place improved MCIF into production
2. Continue strong performance of the duties in the Job Description.

Why you need to understand why your employees are working!

Chapter Nine

Employee Perceptions and Attitudes

"That's my opinion...and by the way, it's yours as well."
Anonymous

"You know the difference between a dead skunk and a dead boss on the road? There's skid marks by the skunk."
Anonymous

Theories on Perceptions and Attitudes

Did you know that what you perceive about issues, whether the issues are right or wrong, will dictate what actions you will take? It is not whether the issue is real or not, it is whether you perceive it to be real that counts.

Emotions are real, powerful, and a compelling force we all have to acknowledge.

If, for example, you perceive that you have been wronged, whether or not it is true, your perception, not reality, will have a lasting impact upon your mental processes. With this in mind, it requires us to understand what causes these perceptions and the attitudes derived there from.

Theories on attitude and perceptions pronounce:

- Not all employees are motivated or see things the same way. Perception is what we see, and attitudes are what we think about what we see.
- Managers have one set of viewpoints and employees have another.
- Managers must try to understand the perceptual world of their employees.

Perceptions and Attitudes Reality

Wouldn't it be nice if everybody saw things the same way? No differences of opinion? No thoughts contrary to universally accepted norm? Well, actually, I would think it would become very boring and all creative thought would stop. There have to be differences of opinion in order for each of us to experience a growth of mental capacities and to stretch our thinking process.

Current politicians who ask, "Why can't we all just get along?" are really stating "Why can't you all just agree with me?" They expect us to fall in line like lemmings jumping over a cliff in unison. Let's give a cheer to those who question, who don't want to run over the cliff and get wet, and ask,"Why should we follow you?" Let's also give a cheer to the management personnel who allow these questions to be asked.

Management in the business world should expect, yes, even encourage ideas that are contrary to those of personnel at a higher level. Employees should be paid for using their brains first, and all other functions as secondary. When employees question, it keeps everyone in the organization on their toes, and *most often adds credibility to the decisions and actions of those in management.*

From the previous discussion one can now see the value of the next action items, which are:

ACTION #2—*Keep employees informed...never lie to them.*

(Perceptions and attitudes are then formed by fact!)

And...

ACTION #3—*Listen! Stop talking! Listen! (You will never learn anything while you are talking.)*

Keep Employees Informed

This is really sound advice. No, really! "Why", you ask, "should I keep my employees informed, when all they are supposed to do is what I tell them to do?" Good point, after all, there is no democracy in the business world. Once all the data is in, analyzed, questioned, revised and put into an action plan, then a decision as to what to do has then been made by management and they should expect all employees to follow. The employees should follow, and they will follow—with the correct attitudes—if they understand why the decision was made; if they are given a view of the forest and not just the trees.

Asking a fellow employee why the company is heading in a particular direction will lead to speculation, gossip and a lack of productivity. Gossip is one of the greatest productivity inhibitors that exist. However, when always presented with the truth, just the facts, employees have no where else to go with the matter and will return to the usual productivity obstructive subjects such as women, men, and sports. Keeping employees informed as to the purpose of decisions brings the ultimate goal of the company to a personal level with the employee. They see how their contribution is needed for personal and joint success. Their perception will then become, "I am needed in order for this to succeed", and their attitude will then reflect this perception.

Listen

Now is the time for self-reflection. Are you ready? Reflect on this—"Have I ever learned anything while I have been talking?" When I am talking, and I'm sure it's the same way with you, and people are listening, or at least I perceive they are, I feel that I could expound on subjects I'm interested in for expanding periods of time—almost non-stop. But when the period of my self-expression is over, who has learned anything? Not me! Just those who were *listening*. If you ever want to learn anything, ask an open-ended question and then listen. You won't have the opportunity to hear your voice or be enlightened by your insight, but you will be educated, edified, and learn about the person who is doing the talking, and about their insight into the question asked. I love to be educated. I even read encyclopedias for entertainment. (Even though it appears to be pretty weird, I do.) Since I can't talk to a book, I'm bound to learn something. So, if you want to learn about ideas, goals, new procedures, customers, markets, etc., just ask your employees and then sit back and be educated…simply by listening.

It is imperative that to learn anything by listening, you must ask questions that need a response other than a yes or no. For instance, if you wanted to know how Bob feels about a new product, don't ask "Do you like the new product?" A yes or no can answer this. Instead, ask, "Tell me how you feel about this new product Bob, and why?" Now your education will begin and for heaven sake, *when the employee or employees are talking to you, don't answer the telephone!* Have someone or something take a message and then return the call at a later time. If it is perceived that you are more interested in talking to the person on the telephone than listening to what they are saying, then perceptions, whether it is true or not, will take over, the employee will become disinterested and you will have lost a golden opportunity for enlightenment.

How Am I Doing Survey

If you really want to know what the perceptions, not necessarily the reality, are of you and your management skills, and you are not faint-hearted, read on. Otherwise skip this portion and go to chapter nine.

Oh good, you stayed! I'm now going to suggest that every couple of years you provide your employees with a chance to give you their own version of a performance review. I like to call this a "How am I doing survey?" (See exhibit III) This survey is done *anonymously* and will open your eyes regarding your management skills. The questions are usually designed to ferret out specific answers on issues that need to be addressed, and could include some of the following:

- Is your supervisor fair?
- Is he or she consistent?
- Does your supervisor listen to your thoughts and ideas?

- Do you feel he or she is concerned with your needs?
- Does he or she provide exact, clear directions?
- Is your supervisor getting in the way of your productivity?

  (It takes a lot of guts to ask that one!)
- Are you provided with the necessary tools to do your job?
- What areas of management do you feel your supervisor should address?

Each question should be followed by a 'please explain section' regardless of the answer.

Believe me, you cannot conclude a survey like this without discovering a great deal of insight into your perceived management skills as well as the abilities of the managers that you supervise.

The results of this survey should be confidentially reviewed with all those in management positions by their immediate supervisor, so that corrective actions, if any, can be taken. Taking no action after it has been pointed out that deficiencies exist defeats the whole process and wastes a lot of time for everybody involved.

I also hope it is plainly understood that although this survey must be anonymous, if someone says some unflattering remarks about you or another supervisor and you think you know who they are, Bob for instance, no action of any kind should be taken against that employee. If you feel some action is warranted, even though this was simply done to help you, then you need to take a look at yourself to see if you should really be in a management position. Management requires a very tough skin. Remember, you asked for it! I also said that a "How am I doing survey" was not for the faint of heart.

If you agree with the Third Principle of Management—a happy employee takes care of our customers and is more productive—then you must pay attention when they speak.

SAMPLE EXHIBIT III
HOW AM I DOING SURVEY

December 2000   BOSS

-------------------------------- --------------------------
Date of Review   Supervisor

|GRADE|

1. Is your supervisor fair?
   Not always - Treats men better than women.   [4]

2. Is he or she consistent?
   No - see #1   [4]

3. Is everyone treated equally?
   No - see #1   [4]

4. Does he or she listen to your ideas?
   He listens, however, he rarely does what I suggest.   [6]

5. Do you feel he or she is concerned with your needs?
   Yes - as long as I do my job.   [5]

6. Does he or she provide exact and clear directions?
   yes- most of the time ⬜ 6

7. Does your supervisor get in the way of your productivity?
   No - He delegates well. ⬜ 5

8. Are you given the necessary tools to do your job?
   yes- I always have what I need. ⬜ 7

9. Do you feel that your supervisor understands what you do?
   yes- He has done this before. ⬜ 7

10. What is your overall rating of your supervisor and why?
    Aside from his unequal Treatment of some of ⬜ 5
    his employees, he is generally a good boss.

Scoring system
1-Unsatisfactory-immediate improvement necessary.
2-Very poor.
3-Poor.
4-Fair.
5-Meets standards.
6-Above standards
7-Exceeds standards.
8-Far exceeds standards.
9-Outstanding.

Total Score ⬜ 5.3

Sum all grades, divide by the # of items graded to arrive at the total score.

Employee Perceptions and Attitudes 57

Chapter Ten

Management of Group Morale

> *"People with high morale are more productive than people with low morale. They put more of their energy into their work, have a greater sense of involvement and responsibility, and get more satisfaction from their work. Low morale depresses productivity. It costs money, sours attitudes, lowers the level of product quality and service. High morale stimulates higher levels of productivity. It reduces costs, improves product and service quality, and makes money."*
>
> Arnold S. Daniels

> *"When I'm unhappy, I can't work. When I'm happy I don't need to work. But when I don't need to work, I'm unhappy."*
>
> Kenneth Tynan

Morale and Productivity

How are you feeling today? How about yesterday, or last week? How do you think you will feel tomorrow? Does a negative answer to these questions, such as bad, lousy, terrible, and so-so have an affect on your job performance? Whether it is mental or physical anguish you feel, when you are down, so is your productivity. Conversely, responses such as great, or terrific or wonderful enhance your productivity. Negative individual feelings such as those above can also affect the group or team that you supervise or work within. It works like the bad apple syndrome, degenerating the enthusiasm and proficiency of everyone around.

Morale Theories

Armed with the knowledge that low morale on the part of an individual member of a team can influence others, it is expedient for management to understand the causes and effects of individual and group morale.

Management theorists have confirmed:

1. The group is one of the most powerful forces a manager can use to improve productivity.
2. The group can also be a source of productivity prevention.

3. Management can never destroy informal work organizations, so it must learn to work with them and have some measure of influence upon them.

Morale Reality

Having dealt with group morale issues all my adult life, I'm now prepared to discuss with you what does work, so now I would like to introduce you to my next item of action, ACTION #4—*There must be equity among peers!*

Equity Among Peers

I have always found that treating an employee at the same level in the organization any differently than his or her associates is courting disaster and will *undo* all other positive accomplishments that have been made. That's a pretty strong statement but I hope it conveys how strongly I feel about this issue. Employees talk to one another. If any are getting special deals, all the others know about it. I know they have been told on numerous occasions that certain issues, such as salary information, should not be discussed with others. But they know! How is one of life's great mysteries, but they find out. Their perceptions and attitudes are affected by this knowledge—information that they are not supposed to have—so they can't discuss this issue with management.

Consistency must be the foundation upon which all management actions are built. Given the same circumstances, disciplining one employee while not another, or acknowledging one employee and forgetting or ignoring an other employee will eventually erode the *base* of the manager's position and will lead to an underlying resentment towards him or her and the company. Trying to get productivity out of this group and taking good care of the customers isn't likely to happen. Pettiness will absorb all rational thought and complaining will rule. So repeat to yourself over and over, "I must be consistent…I must be consistent…!" I hope it sinks in faster for you than it did for me. But once it's there, please don't forget it. Learn from my mistakes, not yours!

The majority expects that rank has its privileges (RHIP), and that certain perks are obtainable at certain levels in the organization. Very few complaints will be forth coming about these perceived injustices because it is felt that they are shared by all in the organization when that level is reached. However, if that level is reached and the associated perks are not forthcoming, then let's get ready to rumble!

For instance, if senior vice-presidents—you can use any title or level in the organization here—are all given company cars and individual parking places, then *all* senior vice-presidents should have these privileges. Not just a few, most, or certain favorites, but all of them. Whether or not a vice-president has a car when all senior vice-presidents have one is not an issue, because a vice-president and a senior vice-president are not peers. However you establish peers in your organization, it is paramount that they all be treated in the same manner.

Now on a cautionary note, be very careful about continuing or nurturing friendships of those who work within your scope of authority. Friendships are wonderful and should never be taken lightly. A good friend is like the air we breathe, they are always needed and should never be taken for granted. However, nourish the friendships outside of office hours and work diligently on a business level to only treat them as you would anyone else. Remember that attitudes are created by perceptions, whether true or not. Also, be aware of the perception that being your friend might lead to the acquisition of certain benefits not normally available to all (i.e. special treatment, bonuses, salary increases, promotions and numerous others.) So when dealing with friendships within an organization, I have two words of advice, "be careful!"

Take Care of Your Employees

Now, let's move on. Another action item associated with the management of group morale is:
ACTION #5—*Take care of the people who work for you.*

What do I mean when I say, "take care of the people who work for you?" Well, for a starter I mean *know who they are,* that they exist in the company to *assist you* in accomplishing your responsibilities, and that they are not there merely to reinforce your importance in the organization. That might sound a little pessimistic about those in management, but remember, I've been there, and I have seen those thoughts in action. The number of people you manage is not a barometer of success. Actually, those who accomplish the most with the least are at the top of the ladder of management abilities.

As a manager, one of the assumptions that you will need to remember is **you can delegate authority to those under you, but you cannot delegate responsibility.** When you dwell on that statement, you then begin to realize that the people who you oversee in an organization have a powerful impact upon your success within the organization.

Become Their Biggest Fan

Understanding the above, let's determine how we can take care of the people in the company who have been given the great opportunity to work under our direction. As a starter, may I suggest that you become the biggest fan for all of your employees? Do this by bragging about them to their peers, your peers, and upper management whenever possible. Such as, "You should have seen what Bob accomplished yesterday…what a great effort!" Believe me, they will hear about it and will respond very auspiciously. Never degrade your employees in front of the same groups. If you have a problem with an employee, the only way it should be handled is via one on one communication with the staff member involved. *Remember that you have the greatest employees in the company, and by association, you will be one of the best managers as well.*

Promote Often

Take every opportunity given to you to promote employees under your leadership. A promotion might consist merely of a new title while doing the same job, moving from one grade to another within the same job description or a movement up the ladder even if it means they will be working for someone else. I would also take the opportunity to see that these promotions are always communicated throughout the organization by way of letters, e-mail or newsletters. On the same note, however, please don't promote on their annual review and then give them the same salary increase they would have received without the promotion. A salary increase should always accompany a promotion and that the promotion should be a separate, distinct event in the life of the recipient. **Make it a big deal!** Everybody wins.

Timely Annual Reviews

While on this subject, please do their reviews on time and put in the effort it deserves. If you can reflect back to a time during your career that a review was not done when it should have been, and "I was too busy" was the excuse, and then it was done poorly, do you remember how you felt? Sadly most employees have had this experience and felt about it the same way that you did. I also never met a manager who likes to do reviews, myself included a while ago, because it seemed like a minor matter and was given the same attention that went along with that perception.

Talk about a misperception! The annual review, and it's attended encouragement, open communication, and hoped for salary adjustment with an update of the IDP is a critical reinforcement to the employee about their performance. If done properly, an annual review should not point out weaknesses that have not been previously pointed out. To wait until the review time to point out deficiencies is doing a disservice to the employee, you, and the organization. Remember that the annual review should be used to document and reinforce what you and the employee already understand. There should be no surprises!

Employee Terminations

What should you do if an employee's performance is not up to standard? Shouldn't you address it during the annual review? Let's discuss these questions after the introduction of the next item of action.

ACTION #6—*Termination of employment should **never** be a surprise!*

Employee terminations! No body likes to do them; no one likes to receive one; yet they are very much a by-product of doing business. With that in mind, there are two ways that termination of employment can be done: it can be done well, or it can be done poorly. When you call an employee into the office for his or her dismissal for performance related issues, and the employee is *surprised,* then you have done an inadequate job of supervision. No simpler measurement of quality for the termination process can be found. So, if they are surprised, may I suggest that you reevaluate how you interact with your employees? Employee terminations, often thought to have a negative affect on group morale, can actually have a positive influence, and can be done well if the following steps are taken:

STEP 1—The employee should receive a verbal, private communication specifying in detail why the employee is not measuring up to acceptable standards. Once this is explained, listen to the employee's response. It may simply be a misunderstanding of expectations. This step will most often correct the problem.

STEP 2—After following step #1 and the problem continues, a written statement outlining the problem and listing a specific corrective action should be signed by both parties, with a copy also being sent to the personnel department. Specific time frames to correct the problem should also be indicated.

STEP 3—If you are at this step, the employee should now be put on immediate probation. This comes with the understanding that the problem will be corrected and that any additional violations will lead to termination of employment.

STEP 4—If steps 1-3 have been taken and the employee still has not corrected his or her problem, then employment of this person in your organization should come to an immediate end.

It will not come as a surprise! It would also be unfair to the employee or his or her peers for employment to continue. Generally, if most employees are told they have a performance problem by their supervisor, and they have the necessary skills to correct it, they will. Those who do not correct the problem after being given a chance will only hurt morale if they stay. Experience shows that morale often improves right after a termination like this has taken place because the peers of the terminated employee know he or she was not pulling his or her weight in spite of opportunities to change.

Management must realize that they are affecting the happiness, aspirations, feelings, and security of more than just the *employee. Decisions made about one employee affect the lives of all the people surrounding them. These actions cannot be done in a capricious or arbitrary manner. **The feelings of the employee must be respected.***

Management of Group Morale 69

Chapter Eleven

Leadership

> *"All progress has resulted from people who took unpopular positions."*
> Adlai E. Stevenson

> *"An two men ride of a horse, one must ride behind."*
> Shakespeare

Leadership has always been a fascinating subject for me. As I am also a history buff, I like to review the characteristics of great leaders, both now, which are few, and in the past, and compare them with my model of a leader.

How do I define a leader? Well, a leader to me is an individual who possesses the following traits:

- A vision of where he or she wants to go.
- A view of how to get there from here.

- A bullheadedness that will not prevent him or her from accomplishing his or her imagination. And the…
- Charisma that compels us to follow his or her lead.

Now from this description, look around at the individuals who have been given the title of leader and see if they measure up to my expectations. You will be surprised how few actually do.

Leaders are not always found at the top of great organizations, religions and countries. Some of the best leaders in fact have no official title at all. Their leadership comes about through a natural ability rather than by having it bestowed upon them. Having a title no more makes a leader than giving wolves clothing to a sheep makes the sheep vicious.

Examples of Great Leaders

Some of the world's great leaders who also had titles given to them and still fit within my definition of a leader would include the following:

POLITICAL

- *Winston Churchill*—While Prime Minister of England, he used his will—and not a lot more—to rally the British people around him and prevented the spread of National Socialism to the British Isles and on to the Western Hemisphere.

- *Chief Joseph*—The Chief of the Nez Perce Indians, he led his people on a thousand mile retreat to resist the incursion into his tribe's land rights by the advancement of western expansion. The hardships were extreme, but his presence and strength provided the salve necessary to endure.

MILITARY

- *Ulysses S. Grant*—As the last commander of the Union forces during the Civil War, he instilled his desire to bring about a swift end to the war into his commanders. He convinced them that the only way it could be done was to find the Confederate army, attack it and defeat it, wherever it was. His steadfastness in this course of action, while wildly unpopular in the North, was cheered by the troops under his command and led to a successful completion of the conflict.
- *Joan of Arc*—A young peasant girl, aged seventeen, who having received visions she believed were from heaven, convinced the King of France to give her command over the King's troops. She immediately led the troops to the liberation of the City of Orleans in 1429, and defeated the English in four other battles. Later wounded, she was captured by the English during an attack on Paris, tried as a heretic and burned at the stake.

BUSINESS

- *Henry Kaiser*—An American industrialist who attracted worldwide attention during World War II by the speed with which he built ships, he ignored the usual methods of building from the keel up, and used assembly line methods. Kaiser's ships were built in separate sections and welded together in a few days.

- *Henry Ford*—He developed the mass-produced "model T" automobile and sold it at a price the average person could afford. He pioneered in the use of assembly line methods. Because of the savings in time and money made by mass production, Ford could offer more cars to the American public at a lower price than anyone before him could.

RELIGION

- *Joseph Smith*—As a young boy of fifteen, he had a vision whereby he claimed to have been visited by Deity and given the keys to the full restoration of the Gospel of Jesus Christ. Amid great and constant persecution, he never recounted his story, formed the now thirteen million members Church of Jesus Christ of Latter-day Saints (Mormons) and was martyred in 1844 by a mob in Illinois.

- *Muhammad*—The founder of the Islamic religion, he is believed to be the last messenger of God and to have completed the sacred teachings of such earlier prophets as Abraham, Moses and Jesus. When he began to preach in the 600's, he replaced lawlessness and the old loyalty to tribes with a new tie of equality and allegiance among all Muslims.

GENERAL
- *George Washington*—As the head of the Armed Forces during America's revolution with the British, and as the first elected president of the new nation, he presided over events that propelled the new nation to greatness. Then at the peak of his glory, he astonished the European countries by doing the unthinkable—he stepped aside and went back to private life so that the country could experience the processes dictated by the newly established constitution.
- *Brigham Young*—As a prominent religious, military and political leader, he led a movement for the successful settlement of the Western states in America that has never been equaled, either before or after. His genius for organization led to the creation of several hundred communities in the Rocky Mountains, most of which are thriving to this day.

Leaders Without Titles

Now that we have addressed leaders with titles, who are the leaders that lead without titles and where can they be found? Genuine leaders do not need titles to lead. They use natural talents that were acquired during their formative years and leadership comes as a natural by-product of their upbringing. These leaders are every where, even in your organization, and through recognition of these talents are often bestowed with titles and bosship. But not always!

The previous discussion now begs the question, are bosses leaders? Can they be? Do they have to be leaders? Are leaders and bosses and managers the same?

A leader by definition, is to *show the way*, whereas a manager *helps you along the way* after the course has been determined; hence, a manager does not need to be a leader, and a leader does not have to be a boss. They can be one and the same, but most often are mutually exclusive of one another.

Leadership Theories

Now with this knowledge firmly planted in our minds, I should now like to present the theories commonly associated with leadership:

- Every group has informal leaders, those people who are followed because they satisfy a need rather than have any direct power from the company to punish or reward.
- Bosship is the power to get things done by using formal and informal leadership.
- Higher productivity is obtained by bosses who display more concern for *people* than they do for production.

Bosses and Reality

If you are the boss, because you have been given the mantle of bosship, you can expect that your wishes will be carried out. Whether you are a leader or not is a mute point, and has no bearing on your expectations. That said, what could one do with the title of boss that has been received?

Let's answer that question by analyzing just what it is that a boss does. According to my understanding, you can expect that a boss should do the following:
- Employ workers.
- Supervise the effectiveness of their work.
- Provide direction so that they can accomplish the company's business plan.
- Reward or punish as needed, and…
- Be accountable for the actions of the supervised employees.

Accepting the previous definition of what a boss does leads us to another important action item that helps a boss regarding the management of his or her employees; i.e. ACTION #7—*Do they know what is expected? Are employees* ***effective*** *as well as* ***efficient?***

While you are pondering the last statement, walk down the hall and ask Bob if he knows what is expected of him. If you are really adventurous, ask him to list his responsibilities in order of their importance. That being done, now come back to your office, call Bob and tell him not to worry, that you were just doing an exercise in management, and then compare his list to your expectations. If they are the same as your expectations, congratulations! You have mastered the *fundamental understanding* of what a boss is and should be rewarded by getting to skip the rest of this chapter and going straight to chapter eleven. Nice job!

Now for the rest of you! Employees under your direction must know what is expected of them. It is critical to their success, your success and the success of the company as well.

Specific Job Descriptions

The most effective way I have found to do this is to have very specific job descriptions for every employee in your organization. (See exhibit IV) It should be reviewed with them before they are hired, after they are hired, and then again every following year on their anniversary date. *In fact, if there are ten duties that form the job description, then the same identical ten items should be on their performance review.* To have items listed on their job description for which they are not accountable is doing a disservice to everyone.

This process insures that employees in the organization know what is expected of them. The job description and the performance review should also be as detailed as possible. I have found most often that perceived problem employees are really a by-product of poor management; i.e. they really don't know what is expected of them, hence their accomplishments are not in sync with their boss who might have other expectations. Don't let this happen!

It is the boss' responsibility to see that the actions of his or her employees are actually accomplishing the things that need to be done. Working hard at *ineffective tasks* only creates tired employees, with little overall results. Working *effectively* for shorter periods of time will beat working long, non-effective hours every time. An employee should not simply be judged by the number of hours they work. They should be judged by what they accomplish during the time worked.

In fact, someone who works longer hours than the norm has never impressed me. They usually have a personal agenda, such as problems at home, and they desire to spend extra time away from their problems. This most often does not produce extra results for the company.

If all the time at work was spent doing *effective* tasks *efficiently*, then one of two outcomes are possible:

1. Less time will be needed to accomplish the task than originally estimated, or…
2. Much more can be done during the same time frame.

As a boss, the choice is yours!

SAMPLE EXHIBIT IV
Job Description
2000

Position-Marketing Analyst Employee—Bob
Grade—D (determines peers)
Salary Range—minimum $28,000
             mid-point $35,000
             maximum $45,000
Work Schedule—Full time, M-F, 8:00AM to 5:00 PM
Education and/or experience: BS degree in related field or four years practical experience.

Position Summary

1. Provides demographic analysis before the introduction of all new products.
2. Analyzes results of all advertising campaigns.
3. Provides monthly market share reports by product by the 10th.
4. Provides monthly product comparison reports by the 10th.
5. Provides market research on request.
6. Provides monthly customer awareness reports by the 10th.
7. Assists the Marketing Director in the preparation of the marketing budget.
8. Compiles monthly results from the telemarketing campaign by the 10th.
9. Assists in the development of new products.
10 Other duties as assigned.

Required Equipment

1. Personal computer 64mb, 6g hard drive, 48x CD, 56k Modem with Internet access.
2. Laser color printer.(duplex)
3. FAX.
4. Cellular Phone.
5. MCIF.
6. ABA people plus, Word, Excel, Powerpoint

SAMPLE EXHIBIT V
Performance Review

December 2000   Bob

Date of Review   Employee

GRADE

1. Provides demographic analysis before the introduction of all new products.
   Analysis is timely and complete. The data provided is highly relied upon.   [6]

2. Analyzes results of all advertising campaigns.
   Shows good analytical skills. The presentation is concise and easy to digest.   [6]

3. Provides monthly market share reports by product by the 10th.
   Reports are done accurately and on time. Nice Job!   [6]

4. Provides monthly product comparison reports by the 10th.
   Same as #3.   [6]

5. Provides market research on request.
   Bob loves to do this and is in strong demand from other departments. Keep up the good work!   [7]

6. Provides monthly customer awareness reports by the 10th.
   Same as #3 [6]

7. Assists the Marketing Director in the preparation of the marketing budget.
   As previously discussed, Bob needs to be more timely with his input to the budget. However, when received, it is well done. [5]

8. Compiles monthly results from the telemarketing campaign by the 10th.
   Same as #3 [6]

9. Assists in the development of new products.
   Bob loves to do this as well and shows good common sense. His insights into the consumer are much appreciated even if they are not implemented. [7]

10. Other duties as assigned.
    Bob doesn't like to do projects other than research. We have discussed this in the past and is trying hard to improve this rating. [5]

Scoring system   **Total Score** [6.0]

1-Unsatisfactory-immediate improvement necessary.
2-Very poor.
3-Poor.
4-Fair.
5-Meets standards.
6-Above standards
7-Exceeds standards.
8-Far exceeds standards.
9-Outstanding.

Sum all grades, divide by the # of items graded to arrive at the total score.

Leadership 83

Chapter Twelve

Participative Management

"Have three people do five jobs but pay them for four."
                                    Arnold W. Donald

"No one pretends that democracy is perfect or all-wise. Indeed, it has been said that democracy is the worst form of Government except all those other forms that have been tried from time to time."
                                    Winston Churchill

The Office Environment

Let's start this chapter off with a bang! The office place is not a Democracy. It does not emulate socialism, communism or any other "ism" that can be found. It more closely resembles a Monarch or fascists state if you like political comparisons. The Board of Directors, Partners and sole proprietors all call the shots, everybody else falls into line and carries out their wishes. This is not bad; it's just the way it works. It is feudalism in form and function.

From all of my historical readings, I have gleaned that the Monarchy is the purest, simplest, and most effective type of political organization: one supreme ruler, quick decisions, no opposition, and simplicity in management…do what I say or else! Kingdoms and empires have prospered and achieved greatness under this form of government. It can and does work well as long as the Monarch has the best interests of the people and the Kingdom at heart. Pity to the populace of a Monarchy who has lost this sense of greatness, who becomes overcome with his or her self-importance. That alone is the major disappointment with this form of government, and direct comparisons can be made to elected officials today. They may begin by feeling they have a sense of duty to the people who elected them, catch an incumbent virus by associating with career politicians, and spend the rest of their tenure trying to get re-elected. The vision of duty is gone, replaced by a "Re-elect me so that I may continue to wallow in the finery attached to my heightened position" attitude.

A monarch gone bad can only be replaced through revolution and bloodshed. A fed-up populace and the vote can replace an elected official. A boss who has been caught up with his or her self can only be replaced by…wait a minute, you can't replace your boss; so you must learn to get along with them and help them acquire the traits they are missing. (Hint: Give them a copy of this book!)

Employees and Production

When I was younger and went to professional seminars, I was amazed at the number of managers who compared their success to the number of employees that they supervised. It was always numbers, and these numbers determined their self-importance. Mysteriously lacking were the figures detailing how much production was derived by the masses under their bosship. How much revenue was generated per employee for the company? How many units per employee were produced? Are these people affected by a virus similar to that of an elected official and doomed to merely counting staff members? I don't think so! They are merely caught up in the current rules of the game and when the scoring changes, so will they.

Well, I hope you will be pleased to know that I'm here to state that the scoring has changed. Just like the shift in the business paradigm, there are statistics available to management as we speak that monitor production by each employee, and credit is given to the manager who can produce the most with the least; hence, more and more emphasis is now being placed on the happiness and contentment of the productive workforce.

Employee Input

In order for a boss to succeed under the new scoring system, an additional approach to management should be found; another arrow in the quiver so to speak. That arrow would be called "participative management." Simply stated, participative management allows employees to have input into the management processes of the company. This input can be in the form of:

- Product design.

- Product selection.

- Operational processes.

- Efficiencies, and…

- Company direction.

As previously discussed, you would be pleased at the insight your employees have if only someone would listen to them.

Theories of Participative Management

To use this form of management you must be acquainted with it's associated theories:

1. Participative management is not management by Democracy. The boss makes decisions after reviewing all means of input.
2. No manager can manage a group successfully without being willing to rely upon the group.
3. The manager who uses participative management techniques is interested in results and lets the employees work out the details.

Participative Management Reality

How do you actually use this type of management? I mean, how does it actually work? The most effective way is to simply ask questions of your staff and then listen—here we go with that theme again—for the results. Don't ever be shy about asking the opinion of the people whom you employ. They all have them-opinions that is—and they want badly to share them with you if they believe you will listen. But you must be ready, willing, and able to listen and to let them know they have been heard.

In my formative years, I attended a national management meeting of all management personnel in the company for which I worked. It lasted three days. On the last day we were asked by the President and CEO to put any questions we had in writing and he would respond to each and every one. We, as a group, had several questions for which we felt we would finally receive enlightenment. Of course, not one employee received a response to his or her question. Why he asked remains a mystery to all of us. That happened decades ago, and yet I still remember this one boss who stated that he was ready to listen, to hear ideas, to give us the chance to provide our insight into the direction of our company, but was unwilling to even give us the courtesy of a response.

Participative Management Actions

If you aren't willing to let the employees share their insights, talents, and thoughts about the business with you and to respond to their ideas, then please don't ask. Being ignored by your boss when one feels that they have some valuable input will eliminate all future input and management will have to provide direction on their own. If you don't agree with some advice, just say so. "I don't necessarily agree with your thoughts on this matter Bob, and here is why… but I sure do appreciate hearing your ideas, they keep me informed." How would you respond if your ideas were turned down as well as this? Think about it? Your employees will respond in the same way. Remember that you are looking for ideas, whence they come is not an issue.

So, with that discussion in our hip pocket, here comes my next item of action (a five pointer no less):

ACTION #8—

1. *Hire the best personnel available.*

2. *Give them the necessary directions.*

3. *Give them the tools to do the job.*

4. *Get out of the way!*

5. *Follow up.*

Hire the Best

If I told you that I have known managers that are unwilling to hire the most talented people because they are afraid that they will eventually be replaced by that person, would you believe me? Of course you would because you have probably seen the same thing. I believe that that concept alone has led to a very ineffective and inefficient mindset throughout organizations that is stifling productivity today.

Marking and protecting one's area-comfort zone—is an inherent trait of most species inhabiting the planet, even Homo sapiens like us. Fences to mark our property, cubicles to define our work area, and boundaries to mark political regions are all samples of this mannerism. It is in our genes and is hard to ignore.

Remember the new scoring system. You're not judged by the number of people you supervise, you're judged by the output that is produced. If you hire the best available, produce more than others, and generate more revenue, how can that negatively affect your comfort zone or career? You will more than likely be promoted because you have capable, talented people to replace you as you move on. If it is your desire to stay where you are, then you are also training and developing employees of the highest level and you will receive the proper recognition. Hiring the most talented individuals is a win-win situation for everyone.

Give Instructions

What about the boss who hires the most talented individuals in the area and then just leaves them alone to ferret out what they should be doing so that he or she can do what they consider more important tasks? "I'm sure they will figure out what they should be doing, they're talented people," this boss will say. If you've heard that in your organization, or something similar, I'll bet it was accompanied by a lot of consternation on your part. Agreed, these people you just hired are good. They are very good in fact, or you would not have employed them. However, they must be guided in very explicit terms as to what is expected of them. That being done, then you can do other things, maybe even play a little golf, and expect that they are moving in the right direction. You owe them that! Merely hiring them without giving them a sense of direction is ludicrous in the extreme. Unfortunately, it is so basic that every one feels it is being done, usually by others, and it is often overlooked. Refer back to ACTION#7—Do they know what is expected? Detailed direction must be given to every employee to achieve the productivity increases promised.

Provide the Necessary Tools

If you have ever worked on a car, done home improvements, crafts or woodworking, you'll understand how easy some procedures become when you use the proper tool. Using a knife as a screwdriver, or a pair of pliers as a replacement for the proper wrench, or duct tape to fix everything are some of my favorite forms of mal-practice. Sometimes, the temptation to miss-use a tool can be overpowering, like the water sprayer in the kitchen sink. For instance, affixing a little scotch tape to the sprayer will cause it to come on when the faucet is turned on. When aimed properly, it can be very amusing to the person who applied the tape; but it is generally not amusing to the person who turned on the faucet. *Warning!...Do not try this at home! This is only for professionals who are trained in its use.* So during my life I have learned one very important tenet—using the properly designed tool to accomplish the proper task is much easier, faster, and better than using substitutes. My motto has become, "The right tool, or not at all." This works especially well when dodging those weekend projects from the job jar that we all have to put up with.

It becomes harder to avoid projects at the office though. The fact that you are paid to do them probably causes this, and if management is on their toes, not having the proper tool is one utterance that should never be heard.

The tools available today in the office environment are very much taken for granted; however, thirty-five years ago it would have stretched the imagination to even conceive of such time saving devices. Some of the tools of the office that have been developed in my lifetime to increase productivity several fold would include:

- The personal computer—The greatest invention since electricity.
- Word processors—Can you imagine typing anything without it?

- Faxes—Once the domain of law enforcement, it is now available to all.
- Internet—The greatest source of information—ever!
- Cellular Phones—In the realm of "Beam me up Scotty!" just a few years ago.
- Scanners—Now the office in Singapore can see what Bob looks like. (They probably wished they never asked!)
- E-mail—Instant communication around the world in seconds.

The tools required to perform the duties listed on the job description and the performance review should be described in the job description itself. (See exhibit VI) In so doing, any omissions of proper tools needed will be discovered when the job description is reviewed with the potential and newly hired employee.

Leave Them Alone

Once the best available employees are in the fold, have received proper direction, and are armed with an arsenal of tools, then may I suggest that you get out of the way! Play golf or something. Leave them alone. Don't interfere! Explain to them what needs to be done, but leave the how up to them. Now would be a great time to do some strategic planning at an off site location. I think you get the picture. In other words, *get out of the way!* If you have done the first three tasks in ACTION#8, then you deserve to go on to something else for a while. Congratulate yourself. You have mastered one of the basic tenets of productive management.

Follow-up

But don't go too far or for too long. One of the caveats associated with delegating authority is that the responsibility still lies with you. So when you come back from the Jazz game, it would behoove you to check with Bob to see how things are going. "How are things going?" you should ask. Bob, I'm sure will say "Fine", and tell you to leave them alone. The point I'm trying to make is once things are set in motion, it is still your responsibility to see that the course is maintained, that you will arrive as scheduled at your destination, with all tasks accomplished, and on budget. That is what management does, and the role you must play. Where you're going, and its associated costs and time frames is up to you; how to get there is up to your staff.

Now sit back, watch, and enjoy how well your employees perform their jobs.

SAMPLE EXHIBIT VI
Job Description
2000

Position—Marketing Analyst Employee—Bob
Grade—D (determines peers)
Salary Range—minimum $28,000
    mid-point $35,000
    maximum $45,000
Work Schedule—Full time, M-F, 8:00AM to 5:00 PM
Education and/or experience: BS degree in related field or four years practical experience.

Position Summary

11. Provides demographic analysis before the introduction of all new products.

12. Analyzes results of all advertising campaigns.

13. Provides monthly market share reports by product by the 10th.

14. Provides monthly product comparison reports by the 10th.

15. Provides market research on request.

16. Provides monthly customer awareness reports by the 10th.

17. Assists the Marketing Director in the preparation of the marketing budget.

18. Compiles monthly results from the telemarketing campaign by the 10th.

19. Assists in the development of new products.

20. Other duties as assigned.

Required Equipment
7. Personal computer 64mb, 6g hard drive, 48x CD, 56k Modem with Internet access.
8. Laser color printer.(duplex)
9. FAX.
10. Cellular Phone.
11. MCIF.
12. ABA people plus, Word, Excel, Powerpoint

Chapter Thirteen

The Management of Change

"Denial is more than a river in Egypt."

C B S TV July 1992

"Change has considerable psychological impact on the human mind. To the fearful it is threatening because it means that things may get worse. To the hopeful it is encouraging because things may get better. To the confidant it is inspiring because the challenge exists to make things better. Obviously, then, one's character and frame of mind determine how readily he brings about change and how he reacts to change that is imposed on him."

King Whitney, Jr.

"He who rejects change is the architect of decay. The only human institution which rejects progress is the cemetery."

Harold Wilson

Change is Constant

I'm sure you have heard the statement that the only sure things in life are death and taxes. Well, I'd like to amend that statement—the only sure things in life are death, taxes and change. See, it's happening already. *In fact, change is about the only constancy there is in life!* Just when you are beginning to feel comfortable about the way things are going at the office—your position, influence, self-actualization, etc.—something always happens to put a damper on your euphoria—a new boss, re-organization, re-engineering, downsizing, a merger or acquisition, technology improvements, and so on. The lists of changes that are happening are endless. If you aren't involved with change at the workplace or at home may I suggest that a check of your pulse be in order.

Change and Theories

The interesting thing about change, and the *key* that drives all theories on the management of change, is *how you or your employees feel about it*. What is my perception of what is happening? How does this affect my comfort zone? What is the impact on the forces driving me to work here? In other words, how does this affect me?

Change analysts (there are experts everywhere these days) have postulated about change as follows:

- Change is common. (The money spent to reach this result will stagger the mind.)

- The objective of management during periods of change is to maintain the equilibrium that the change is upsetting.

- Management must manage the process of eliminating the barriers to accepting change.

- Two-way communication well in advance helps reduce the individual's resistance to change.

Change and Reality

I think that we can establish that you and I are fairly insightful and normal people. You're showing great insight by reading this book for instance, while I showed great insight by…well, you be the judge. Sometimes it is just remarkable to be normal. Not exclusive, not sub-anything, but normal! Do you know that how you respond and react to certain stimuli in the workplace is fairly consistent with how others will respond? You can use yourself as a fairly accurate measurement when it comes to responding to change in the office. Think about how enlightening it is to understand how others in your employ will feel about forthcoming changes.

With that understanding, the next action item should now be obvious:

ACTION #9—*Treat employees as you would want to be treated.*

It's so simple and so obvious that I had to wrestle with myself to include this action in this book. "Everybody knows this and are probably tired of being reminded of it," I thought. But in retrospect, since I did include it, I must have pinned myself while wrestling; or it could be that I thought if everybody knows this, then why aren't they doing it? It was actually for the last reason it was included. I don't know how to wrestle very well.

The Communication of Change

If you don't think you feel the same way as others in your employ, then ask Bob how he feels about the communication given to all employees during the last episode of change. You'll find out that you think more like Bob than you ever thought you would or hoped you would for that matter. (Cheer up, it's not that bleak!) After that, let's discuss some changes that are happening or potentially will happen in your workplace and review your responses; hence, the responses of your employees as well to these changes.

In the past, when a change happened in the workplace, how did you hear about it? Did it come through the rumor mill? How about from a source outside of the company or from the media? Did you hear about it from a sub-ordinate or a peer? A newsletter perhaps, or right from the top? However you heard about it, please stop and reflect about how you felt about the way the change was communicated to you and the organization. Don't think about the change itself, only the way in which you were told. If you feel good about it, then chances are if the rest of the employees heard about it in the same manner, then they will feel good about the way the change was communicated as well. If so, you have discovered a process of communicating change that should be documented for future use.

If you heard about it one way, and the rest of the staff another, put yourself in their shoes and then ask yourself if you would be contented with the results. Again, use yourself as a yardstick.

If it were your duty to inform your employees of the change, the same method of self-analysis would apply. Anticipate the questions you would ask if you were in their place and make sure those questions are answered during your presentation.

- How does this affect me in my work habits, or my personal goals, or driving factors, benefits, salary, incentive pay, hours worked, and personal satisfaction?

- How will the change come about?

- When will it happen?

- Why?

- How does it affect our customers?

- What type of training, if any, will it involve?

If you've answered all of the questions you would have to your satisfaction, then you should feel good about announcing the changes to all concerned.

It is also important that everyone hear about the changes in the *same manner* and at the *same time*. *Consistency during this process is very important.* If this doesn't happen, then the rumor mill will take care of it for you. Unfortunately, however, most of what will be discussed there will be wrong.

I'll always remember a meeting I attended in Atlanta one year that brought the senior management from several banks together to talk about the changes that were happening and expected to happen in the Financial Services Industry. As we were discussing change, the question was asked as to how many believed their organization would be acquired by another bank during the next few years. About eighty percent of those gathered said that they felt that they would merge with another bank, or possibly, acquire one itself.

One particular banker, the President and CEO of a small bank in the Midwest, said that his bank had no intention whatsoever of becoming involved with what he termed "merger mania." While he had the floor, he used his time to scold all of those bankers present and presented a short discourse on the evils of having just a few larger banks instead of several smaller ones.

After that session, he called the bank to get messages, as everyone does, and was informed that the bank had been sold that morning to an out of state bank as directed by the Chairman of the Board and the majority stockholder. Of course, he was devastated. Not only did his worst fears come true, but he was left out of the negotiations as well. His biggest grievance to this change though was the manner in which he was informed. If the Chairman of the Board had only asked himself how he would want to be informed of the sale if he were the President and CEO, then at least the self-respect of that employee would have remained intact.

Unfortunately, for whatever reason, he did not ask the question of himself.

Look Inward Before Counseling Others

Treating your employees, as you would want to be treated works extremely well in all facets of employee management, not just with the management of change.

When dealing with an employee, for whatever reason, simply ask yourself how you would want to be treated if you were they. **Answer the following questions about yourself before providing counsel to others:**

- How would I want to be informed of a performance problem?

- How would I want to be acknowledged for a job well done?

- How would I want to be told of new responsibilities?

- How would I want to be told about reduced responsibilities?

- How would I want to be given my annual review?

- How would I like to be informed of a promotion?

The list of questions could go on, but I'm sure the point has been made. You are a tremendous resource of information on how to deal with others, just waiting to be tapped. I'd strongly suggest that now is the time to plug it in.

This principle is so very basic, yet so important in business as well as our everyday lives. You can't escape interaction with people; they are everywhere, even at the office and in your neighborhood. Just remember to *look within yourself before advising others.*

Chapter Fourteen

Just Be Nice

"The greater man, the greater courtesy."

Tennyson

"Politeness costs nothing and gains everything."

Lady Mary Worthy Montagu

"To speak kindly does not hurt the tongue."

French Proverb

Today's Society

If I were to view society today through the eyes of the media, especially television, I would come to the conclusion that civility is no longer practiced. Gaining influence and power by whatever means possible is the norm that is presented. Even businesses advertising their products are caught up in this distortion, and are adding to this missconception. One particular commercial that I find most offensive (I can't even remember the product so it really isn't very effective) consists of two people actually licking the shoes of their boss so that they might receive a promotion. One of the lickers uses the advertised product, hence receives the promotion and has now become the lickee of the other licker. To promote the notion that one must lower themselves to this level makes me ill. To even acknowledge that a boss would want this to happen, and would actually encourage it and allow this to happen makes me sad. The old saying, "nice guys finish last" seems to be the motto of the day!

To emphasize this all the more, in all of my study and research, I was unable to find any theories that dealt with courtesy towards your employees and its impact upon job performance. I find this to be incredulous. *To ignore the relationship between a happy employee, caused simply through an act of civility, and productivity accompanied by exceptional customer service is, I believe, utter nonsense.* So, it is on this enlightened note that I avow how wrong and ignorant this belief is.

The Art of Being Nice

That presents a great opportunity to now furnish the last and simplest of my ten action items: ACTION #10—*Above all else, just be nice!*

"Okay, what does this mean, and what do I need to do?" I'm sure are some of the questions you now have; or as former President of the United States Bill Clinton would say, "Define nice."

Well to me, being nice is synonymous with being courteous and polite to *everyone*. I emphasize *everyone*, and not just a select few. That being said, let's discuss some very specific methods of being nice in the workplace. (Remember, there is no cost to this action, only rewards.)

Remember the cauliflower incident involving Bob? Yep, that one. Talk about being upset! I remember that you wanted to do him bodily harm over that. But as I recall, you refrained, walked away, and dealt with the issue the next day after having cooled off. Bob also had to deal with it for twenty-four hours so when the time came to discuss it with him, you simply had to point out the error of his ways, why it was wrong, and why it was in his best interest to never let it happen again. Had you addressed the issue while you were angry, words would have been said that you both would have regretted later. In short, part of being nice would be to *never address an employee or an associate while in a fit of anger*. Back off and let cooler heads prevail later. *A word spoken in anger is like a tattoo; it makes you feel good at the time, but it is hard to erase later and leaves irreparable scars.*

How do you feel when you've been ordered or commanded to do something? Unless you are in the Military or have a low dose of self-esteem, I can accurately predict that you will be annoyed. Sometimes annoyed enough to cause physical harm to some of your office supplies. Remember that you are a measurement. If you feel that way, so will others. So when a direction is given in the source of a question with a universally accepted "please", the results are predictable. Re-phrasing commands into a question is easy. Instead of saying"Get that report for me"; you would replace it with "Would you please get that report for me?" The results will be the same. So if your desire is productivity, and you believe that happy employees are more productive, then **ask nicely and you will receive…but demand and you will also receive, but with acrimony.** Oh, and by the way, when it is received, please say "thank you". This is pretty good advice offered by one of the most prominent men in the field of employee productivity… which would be…ah…me again! You are now treating employees as people, not indentured servants, and believe me, they will respond positively and productively. Isn't that why they were hired in the first place?

Now I've found that this treatment works well for every type of employee except for *career* politicians. They just don't respond properly. Here we are, actually giving them money during the interview and hiring process, then they are hired, given a salary, great benefits, perks that we would all die for and then we are pretty much ignored. We only hear from them again when the hiring cycle begins anew. The only effective way I have found to deal with them is to start the employee termination process the minute they are hired. Then don't get discouraged because the process takes awhile. Everybody else I've met though acts normally to civility and responds in kind.

Employees and Mistakes

There is one thing that I'm sure we will all agree upon: our employees are not perfect and will make mistakes. (Bob! Need I say more?) They will make mistakes and I'm sure are making mistakes as we speak; so they need support from you during this process because they don't take these mistakes lightly, and the manner in which these mistakes are handled can and will hinder productivity in the future if it is not done with concern for the offender. (Refer to Action #6 for repeated errors.) During this process, think about how you would want to be treated under the same circumstances and act in kind. You cannot go wrong. And remember, civility should be administered at all times.

Other Ways to be Nice

Being nice can also be manifested in other ways. Acknowledging that everyone has problems in their life does this. I mean everyone. Understanding that these problems may manifest themselves while at the office allows us to treat all of our fellow workers with compassion. So *listen when they talk to you*. You probably will not have any answers, but simply listening to them sometimes helps lift the burden they are carrying. But it is important that however you respond, all must understand that you will respond to them in the same manner. If you aren't willing to listen to everyone who wants to discuss his or her problems with you, then may I suggest that you listen to none? Remember that everyone should be treated as equals. You can't afford to be selective, nor should you be.

Being Nice and Giving Gifts

I'm sure you feel that giving gifts and having parties is also a way to be recognized as being nice. Birthdays, promotions, anniversaries, weddings, the birth of children and Christmas are wonderful opportunities to show your employees that you are pleasant. However, here I go again popping your balloon, may I again suggest that if you can't do it for everyone, then please do it for none. Failure to give a gift, or have a party for anyone at the office, while remembering some, brings the "equity among peers" situation into play again. Giving gifts to employees could lead to inadvertent hurt feelings; hence, avoid it. *Having respect for the employee and treating them as an equal will have far greater **lasting** impact upon an employee than will a gift of dubious value.* Respect is also something that can be universally given to all of your employees equally without concern for discrimination by an oversight.

Give It a Shot!

I hope I have addressed Mr. Clinton's request for a definition of being nice in the office. As you can see, these were all subjects taught to you by your parents and drilled into you long ago. Just don't let your position of boss interfere with their execution. Although all ten action items are easy to implement, Action #10 has got to be the easiest. So, if it is your desire to ignore the other nine, please, if all else fails, *Just Be Nice!*

While you're pondering this, picture two squirrels in a tree, and one squirrel says to the other, "how will you ever know whether you're a flying squirrel if you don't give it a shot?"

Well! Go on! Give it a shot!

Chapter Fifteen

Conclusion

"It was the best piece of advice I ever ignored."
                                              Edward R. Murrow

"When I was a boy of fourteen, my father was so ignorant I could barely stand to have the man around. But when I got to be twenty-one, I was astonished at how much the old man had learned in seven years."
                                              Mark Twain

Thirty-five Years of Experience

Well, there you have it. Thirty-five years of experience and research on my part condensed into about two hours of reading on your part. But wait, I'm not done there! If you call in the next ten minutes, you will receive…oops, sorry…wrong media. Actually, I've consolidated the book down even further because times are often hectic at the office. Inspite of myself, I need to continually remind myself and others about how I feel about employee treatment lest I forget during all the commotion. I did this by taking the following analysis of management etiquette and having it enlarged to poster size, framed and hung on the wall in front of my desk for all to see, especially me. It became a constant reminder of how I feel and what I believe, and a great conversational tool as well. So here it is:

A ONE MINUTE ANALYSIS OF MANAGEMENT ETIQUETTE

Principle #1—The single greatest key to productivity is happy employees.

Principle #2—Employee treatment is the key to employee happiness.

Principle #3—Happy employees take care of our customers and are more productive.

Principle #4—Happiness in employment comes from achieving one's employment goals.

Principle #5—Helping people achieve employment objectives creates happy employees; hence, productive employees.

Therefore:

Action #1—Understand why people are working and commit to help them achieve these goals.

Action #2—Keep employees informed…never lie to them.

Action #3—Listen! Stop talking! (You will never learn anything while you are talking.)

Action #4—There must be equity among peers.

Action #5—Take care of the people who work for you.

Action #6—Termination of employment should never be a surprise!

Action #7—Do they know what is expected from them?

Action #8—Hire the best—Give directions—Give them tools—Get out of the way—Follow up.

Action #9—Treat employees as you would want to be treated.
Action #10—Above all else, BE NICE!

A Reminder

I hope you have been enlightened and enriched by my suggestions. As I promised, there isn't much new here, but it is a reminder to all those currently in management positions and to those aspiring to be, that treating an employee *justly*, *equally* and *respectfully* will have a significant impact upon your bottom line, as well as your soul; and it is also the cheapest form of productivity enhancement known to man, since the only cost is an effort on your part. So, may I offer this last piece of advice? Go on… try it…you'll like it!

INDEX

action, 7, 9, 13, 15, 29, 33, 35-36, 39-41, 48-49, 52, 60, 62-63, 66-67, 72, 76, 90, 92, 95, 102, 110, 112, 114, 117-118
annual review, 64-66, 106
Bob, 13-14, 20, 23, 26, 41, 50, 52, 63, 76, 79, 89, 94-96, 103, 110, 112
bosship, 75-76, 86
Business Hierarchy, 4-6, 10-12
communities, 4-5, 74
Consistency, 61, 104
customers, 4-6, 8, 15, 17-21, 28, 50, 53, 61, 104, 117
driving factors, 23, 39, 104
Employee terminations, 66
employment goals, 23-25, 27-28, 117
employment treatment
etiquette, 3-4, 6, 8, 10, 12, 14, 18, 20, 24, 26, 28, 32, 36, 38, 40, 42, 44, 48, 50, 52, 54, 56, 60, 62, 64, 66, 68, 72, 74, 76, 78, 80, 82, 86, 88, 90, 92, 94, 96, 98, 100, 102, 104, 106, 110, 112, 114, 116-118
friendships, 62
happy employees, 13-16, 19-21, 26, 28, 111, 117
Hierarchy of Needs, 8
How am I doing survey, 51, 53
individual development plan, 39
leaders, 70-71, 74-75

listen, 48, 50-51, 66, 87-89, 113, 117
management, 3-4, 6-8, 10, 12, 14-15, 17-18, 20-21, 24, 26, 28, 32-33, 36-38, 40, 42, 44, 48-54, 56, 58-69, 72, 74, 76-78, 80, 82, 84-107, 110, 112, 114, 116-119
Maslow, 7, 23
mentors, xi
morale, 9, 33, 38, 58-63, 65-67, 69
motivating factors, xii
participative management, 33, 84-85, 87-89, 91, 93, 95, 97
personal issues, 18
poor customer service, 9, 20
practices of correct behavior, 6
predictive index, 38-39
productive employees, 26, 28, 117
productive workforce, 86
productivity, 4, 6-9, 13, 15-18, 20, 25, 27-28, 35-36, 38, 49, 52, 58-59, 61, 75, 90, 92-93, 109, 111-112, 117, 119
profitability, 4-5, 9, 25, 28
promote, 38, 64, 109
rank has its privileges, 61
reality, 7, 31-33, 36, 47, 51, 60, 76, 88, 102
shareholders, 4-5
specific job descriptions, 77
stakeholders, 5
theories, 4, 7, 31-33, 35-36, 46-47, 59, 75, 88, 101, 109

Printed in the United States
69703LV00001B/68